Finding Your Career Niche

Finding Your Career Niche

Conversations About Women & Business

Anne S. Klein

BUSINESS EXPERT PRESS

Leader in applied, concise business books

Finding Your Career Niche: Conversations About Women & Business

Copyright © Business Expert Press, LLC, 2021.

Cover design by Charlene Kronstedt

Interior design by Exeter Premedia Services Private Ltd., Chennai, India

First published in 2021 by
Business Expert Press, LLC
222 East 46th Street, New York, NY 10017
www.businessexpertpress.com

ISBN-13: 978-1-95334-954-5 (paperback)
ISBN-13: 978-1-95334-955-2 (e-book)

Business Expert Press Business Career Development Collection

Collection ISSN: 2642-2123 (print)
Collection ISSN: 2642-2131 (electronic)

First edition: 2021

10 9 8 7 6 5 4 3 2 1

Printed in the United States of America.

Dedicated to my husband, Gerhart L. Klein, Esq., for all his love and assistance researching and editing this book.

And to my late parents, Dr. Charles B. Sceia and Kathryn Lucas Sceia, whose love and guidance gave me the education and courage to succeed in my career and to write this book.

Special acknowledgment to Kayla Bertolino, my neighbor and young friend whose insight was invaluable as I wrote this book.

Description

This book is a conversation—not a lecture—for women. If you are wondering how to approach your career (at any age) and how to decide when the time is right to have children, there are questions for you to help you decide. Gender inequality and bias issues continue to have relevance for women as they did back in the mid-1960s. Fortunately, legal cases brought by many courageous women over the years have resolved some of those issues. Other chapters in this book give women additional perspectives on networking, surviving in the corporate environment, and entrepreneurship.

Keywords

career choices; networking; gender inequality; sexual bias; entrepreneurship

Contents

Preface

In this book, *Finding Your Career Niche—Conversations About Women & Business,* I share my 50+ years of experience in the corporate and entrepreneurial worlds. Women can pursue business careers, as long as they understand the challenges in their future. I include several checklists to help you determine your career path. There are other checklists to help women decide when to have children, how to network, and when it is time to start a business.

In my first book, *On the Cusp: The Women of Penn '64* (coauthored with Vilma Barr), we tell the stories of 19 University of Pennsylvania women graduates who had few, if any, female role models to follow. They achieved success on their own, with no career path and little guidance to help develop their talents. In *"On the Cusp,"* many of our female classmates told incredible stories about the obstacles they faced during their journeys into the worlds of business, law, medicine, science, government, and public service. Feminism, the glass ceiling, networking, and female entrepreneurship were as yet unknown concepts.

Gender inequality wasn't a topic even discussed in the 1960s. Women had "their place" in business and in our society. With our good education and the confidence we had, we thought we could do anything. We never thought if we "hit a wall," the wall was there because of our gender.

In the 1970s, women thought they had to do it all: marriage, family, career, children, whatever—the Superwoman concept. In *Finding Your Career Niche*, you will see you have a choice.

None of us—The Women of Penn '64—ever made it to the CEO level in a major corporation. The business and societal environment had not yet progressed far enough. Yet, many of us became CEOs of our own companies. We have reached out and helped others. Like the pioneers, we blazed the trails so other women could follow.

In this book, we revisit some of the issues we faced in the mid-1960s and discuss how they affect women today and how you can avoid them.

CHAPTER 1

Strategies for Advancing in Your Career

As I was growing up in the 1950s, my parents often assured me that I could be anything I wanted to be. In that era, women's rights and women's equality were still largely unknown concepts. In most cases, men were the breadwinners; women were expected to become wives and mothers. Those who did enter the workforce typically became secretaries, teachers or nurses. But my parents instilled in me a belief that I not only would go to college, but that I should expect to go to one of the world's most prestigious business schools, the almost exclusively all-male Wharton School at the University of Pennsylvania. And I did, entering the school in the fall of 1960. When I got there, though, I quickly noticed I was the only woman in nearly all of my classes (other than only a few women in large lectures).

My First Dose of Reality

Early on, I received a sad dose of reality. In the fall of my freshman year, the sociology graduate assistant was prone to making sexist comments. He was so unsubtle that eventually even the guys in my class called him out and made nasty comments to him when he went "over the top." To their credit, my male classmates were protective, and I was grateful.

Many of the professors and instructors were not ready for women in the classroom. For example, in my senior year at Wharton, there was a protestant minister who taught a course called "Marriage and the Family." It was considered a "gut" course, that everyone should easily pass. Looking back, it was clear the degree of bias the minister brought to that class. His demeanor and reaction when he saw me in the class were a dead giveaway. He had an arrogance about him that was upsetting to me. All the men received an A or B grade, but I received a C grade. So much for a "gut" class. Despite the fact I had straight As in all my other classes that year, I received the lower "C" grade in "Marriage and the Family." (By the way, I have been married for 44 years now, so I suppose I have overcome whatever deficiencies this minister perceived in me!)

After my sophomore year at Wharton, I was required to choose a major. I wanted this major to be in corporate finance. Most corporate finance majors later went on to work on Wall Street and made a lot of money. But I soon learned that I would not be *allowed* to major in corporate finance. The chairman of the department declared, "*No woman will ever receive a degree in corporate finance as long as I'm in charge.*" I had to settle for my second choice—marketing. This major was still in the Wharton School, where I ultimately received my bachelor of science degree in economics.

Opportunities Today

Today, of course, women can do whatever they have the skills for and desire to be—like an airline pilot or a ship captain, an information technology professional, a lawyer, a doctor, or even a corporate finance professional on Wall Street. The opportunities today are so plentiful and varied that they often cause confusion.

At this stage of my life, I am often asked by young women to give them advice on choosing a career. For those who ask, I walk them through the following exercise I developed. There is nothing mystical about this process; it is the same type of decision analysis you might use to determine what kind of vacation you would like to take.

Deciding on Your Career

One of the ways to start is by making a list of your personality characteristics. Do you enjoy working alone or with others? What other personality characteristics do you have? Make a list of what you are truly like as a person. Then, do a web search for "women and careers" to see which of the many available career choices intrigue you. Here is one website that I think is very helpful: www.CareerGirls.org/explore-careers/careers.

Then, compare your personality characteristics with those of the careers. Be honest with yourself, because you can be choosing a life-long career.

Are you a competitive person? For example, if you play basketball or softball or tennis or some other sport (whether a team or individual sport), how important is it for you to win? Or are you not the competitive type? If you like winning, then you might enjoy working on a team that is challenged to develop new products or services. If not, you might prefer a job where you work mostly on your own or where your team is expected to be productive but not necessarily innovative.

Then, ask yourself the same questions about careers you think you'd like to pursue. Is the career path one that allows you to work alone? Or does the career involve your interaction with others? How often would you have to interact with others?

If there is no major difference in what you think you'd like to do (consider your personality traits) and the career path you have chosen, then you should pursue that choice. If there is a major difference in your personality traits and the career path you have chosen, then you probably should rethink this career path.

If you are an engineer, why would you want to pursue a career in art? There is a disconnect here.... If you are so creative, then maybe you need to get a master's degree in art, and combine the two majors to pursue your career. Maybe you can design a new system to discover art forgeries. Or just be an engineer whose passion is art.

In addition to an assessment of your personality and your potential career, here is another technique that will help you evaluate the pros and cons of the job. Use the effort/impact grid. This analysis will tell you if you can invest the time required to be an attorney or a physician, or if you should work for your PhD. If you can invest the time, what type of return will your investment bring to you in the future?

Search the "Want Ads"

One of my friends told me she would try to determine what the latest "hot" careers were by looking in the *New York Times*' help-wanted ads or, today, online at such sites as LinkedIn, Glassdoor, ZipRecruiter, and a host of others. Then she chose a career that would fit with her personality characteristics. She took courses in college—math and statistics—so that she could build her career. She also took courses that made her happy (liberal arts) and were in line with her personality. (My friend's mother wanted her to be a teacher; she didn't like teaching, so she pursued her degree as a sociology major, began as an employment counselor, then moved on to business.)

Once you have gotten an idea of the available career options, make a list of those options that appeal to you.

Then ask yourself a series of questions:

- How do you want to spend your life?
- What is important to you?
- Do you want to "have it all"?
- Do you thrive on having a lot to do?
- Or are you the type of person who wants a relaxed environment?

In other words, would your ideal career involve high stress (and, ideally, commensurate high pay) or are you willing to sacrifice some of your earning potential for a career that is more easy-going and less stressful? Would you be happy in a job that requires 60 to 80 hours a week, or will you be satisfied to be a nine-to-five-er? Or perhaps something in between?

Changing Your Career Path

By the way, if you are just starting out, don't think the career path you choose now has to be for all time. If you think you will be happy in one career and then discover you really dislike that career choice, change it. After being a volunteer for many years and married to a doctor, a friend returned to college for a master's degree. After many different jobs getting back into the work force, my friend found an opportunity to work with a college chancellor. Several of my college classmates took advantage of opportunities to switch their careers. One finished her degree in architecture because she decided she wanted to head an architecture department, and not be a draftsman all her life.

Another classmate took advantage of her English degree, pursued a master's degree and taught an English language course in Asia.

Many people change not only their jobs but also their careers; some do it several times in their lifetime. This is where your adaptability comes into play. Even if your education is fairly narrow in its subject scope, there are still a number of different paths you can take. For example, if you are a biology major, you could become a physician or a microbiologist or a researcher or any of a number of different career paths that include biology as a starting point. If you have a broader, less specific education, your career choice is that much broader. It can include almost anything for which you have (or can learn) the basics. One woman, who eventually became a doctor, majored in French; another doctor loved art and took many classes in the subject. Another classmate of mine, at the urging of a friend, took a class in electrical engineering and wound up working for General Electric, in the space program. She was a chemistry major!

Can you survive by taking STEM (Science, Technology, Engineering and Math) courses? Take a look at the women portrayed in the movie and the book *Hidden Figures.* Yes, you need courage like those women, who had to be the best at what they did in a traditional, white-male-dominated environment.

Turning Your Volunteer Efforts Into A Career Path

What you do and when you do it are questions you will face when you want to enter the work force. If you've spent any amount of time volunteering during your days at home as a mom or a nonworking wife, you can use that experience as a fill-in for industry experience. Make sure you keep track of your volunteer work: the responsibilities you were given, the budgets you were responsible for, the personnel you managed, the goals you accomplished, and your experience as a leader.

You can then relate that experience to the job you are seeking. You probably won't have to return to college unless you find you want to enter a completely different field from the one where you were a volunteer.

If the hiring person doesn't value your volunteerism, you should re-evaluate the company where you are applying for the job, especially if the company is involved in the field where you volunteered. Consider alternatives, like community relations or philanthropy for a university or a different corporation.

A Man's Job?

It is no longer unusual for women to work in what used to be "men's jobs." Nor is there any stigma attached to whether you choose a white-collar or a blue-collar career. In fact, careers as an electrician or plumber are in great demand. If you don't want an intellectual career, where you will be continually challenged, maybe you would be happier with other careers that don't require you to be independently creative all the time, but will challenge you in other ways. Choose whatever path you want to take. No matter what your career, you may have to *invest in continuing education* along the way. *The world is changing quickly, and knowledge in virtually every career is constantly evolving.*

If you're not ready to build a career but feel that you must work either to support yourself now or in the future, or to make your parents happy, you will have to keep that in mind too. I wrote a book about 19 of my classmates who graduated from Penn in 1964. While most of these women eventually moved on to other careers that made them happier, many of them got their teaching certificates—most at the urging of their mothers—so they would always have something to fall back on. Teachers back then (in the 1960s) usually received a steady paycheck, and the idea of a regular paycheck was a much sought-after goal for parents in guiding their daughters. Parents of that era were not accustomed to thinking about women in "unorthodox" careers, like being a doctor, an attorney, or an entrepreneur.

Near Home or Far Away?

Mothers in the 1960s did not want their daughters to live too far away from their home—a hundred miles generally was the outer limit. Ask yourself if you are you a homebody? Are you tied to your hometown? I realized I didn't want to be too far from my parents or cousins. So after college, I stayed in Philadelphia, about an hour's drive away from home. It took me four months to get my first job. It was, in fact, the only job that opened up for me, but I had to get started somewhere, even though I didn't know much about the company that eventually hired me. Looking back, not finding out about the company was not the smartest move I could have made, but I needed to get started in my career.

Would you mind living in a different place? Do you enjoy meeting new people? Do you have the urge to travel and see the world? Do you easily make new friends? Perhaps you could look for a job outside of your home market where there is a need for your services or a need for the skills you have to offer. Whatever your chosen career, there are numerous career options for you in many places in the country or even outside the United States.

The career path you choose will have to be YOU—this career path will reflect your personality and you have to be comfortable with this decision.

Understand Your Future: What Can You Do For My Company?

At the request of a family member, I once interviewed a young woman who told me she was majoring in "popular culture." When I asked her what that entailed, she couldn't explain it to me. I really wanted to learn about this major, but I got nowhere in the interview. I learned from this interview that a student has to understand her major. She will be asked more than once about her major. When I asked her what type of job she would be interested in, she could not tell me in words I could understand. Then, I asked her how she planned to use the major in her future. Maybe it was my failing, but I could not understand what she described.

Therefore, be sure you understand your major, especially if you are applying for a position that might be the focus of your life. And most of all, you have to be aware of the interviewer's understanding of what your focus in life is. Pop culture was a "hot" career in the early 2000s, but ask yourself, what can you do with this major in the future? Will you be limited by the timeframe of the courses you took? Be prepared to respond to a question, "What can you do for me (or my company) with your major?" If you can easily explain your major to a prospective employer, you will be fine with your choice. I simply could not understand what this young woman was majoring in and what she planned to do with this major.

You should be careful about majoring in what is "hot." Do not allow the vagaries of current trends to determine your lifetime career choice. And try to make sure the subject you study in college is one that has jobs available after you graduate. Majoring in Medieval English Literature may be something you really enjoy, but there are precious few jobs available. One Eastern European country has forbidden colleges to offer a women's studies major, since there aren't any jobs available. Even in the United States, there are few jobs available for women's studies majors, unless you want to join a university or counsel women. If there are limitations to your career choice, then take classes that give you a broader choice of options.

One of the "hot" careers in the 2020s is entrepreneurship. If you think you want to begin your own business with a great idea, then you will need to take courses in finance, accounting and marketing, which are skills you will need to run a business. Other important skills you will need in starting a business are management and psychology classes, especially if you need to hire employees. When I started my business, I had to learn management and psychology "on the job" because I didn't have any training in these areas. Like me, you may not have the luxury of hiring a human resources person at first.

The Career That Makes You Happy

Then, *there is the consideration about how much you want to work.* If you are pursuing a career until you meet Mr. Right, or to make your parents happy, **consider a career that makes YOU happy**. You don't know when Mr. Right will come along or how many years you will need or want to work. Think about spending your lifetime in a career. How much money can you make for retirement? Will you have to depend on your family to help you out? This is an important decision for you to make, because you want to support yourself for life or through a divorce or as a widow, if you have to.

Select the classes in college that will help prepare you for your future endeavors. If you want to major in a foreign language or humanities, be sure what your future career might be. If you don't understand information technology, then the world might pass you by. With the Covid-19 virus, for example, you might have to work from home, and teachers will have to know how to teach classes online and understand technology. My experience has taught me this fact about technology as the new reality. That technology class that you intensely disliked in school might be your savior. There are so many webinars online, using Zoom or Skype or other platforms. An understanding of these technologies is invaluable. Even parents who find themselves home-schooling their children have to understand the computer and its offerings.

If you decide to start your own business, be sure you have a product or service that you are confident the world needs. Don't look at Mark Zuckerberg or Jeff Bezos as role models. Not every business will be a blockbuster that makes you a billionaire. Take a look at all the work that goes into building a business. Take it from someone who ran a business for 35 years: you work early in the morning until late at night. When the business hits a downturn, you will be the person who takes the hit on income. (My husband and I went without any salary for a year in the recession of 2009 in order to pay our staff. Even our senior vice president took a 50 percent pay cut. We suggested he choose the morning or the afternoon to work. Maybe I should have laid off some staff, but I did not let them go out of a sense of responsibility. The next year, we did all right.) Don't expect that you will make a lot of money without working very hard and making some sacrifices early on.

A college friend started working as a secretary (yes, she did) in a large company that had great benefits. She got married just out of college, and when baby number two came along, she could not stay at that company, even with the excellent benefits. Baby number two needed her attention. But she had other skills she could call upon and she started a retail business in her home; then she moved to a larger office when she had an idea for the fashion industry. After doing her research, she found she could sell her idea, and it was an idea that required extensive travel. (As she aged and couldn't travel as much, she sold her business to her business partner.) She advised women to marry a husband who shares your interests and supports you. She said that she could not have been a success without her husband's support. She also said she would have been a terrible mother if she had not worked for herself. She reports her children turned out just fine.

After more than a decade of marriage, another friend was divorced at an early age. She had married a week after she graduated from college. At the time, she worked as a teacher but she had to leave when she became pregnant. This was the 1970s and women often were not allowed to be obviously pregnant on the job. My friend was creative and I guess you could say she was bitten by the entrepreneurial bug. She developed an idea where she did not have to physically appear in classes, thereby keeping her out of sight of students. Her idea was quite successful. She gave the students community projects they could manage on their own. Then, she moved on and enjoyed working for a not-for-profit agency. When she was asked to write a book and was given no credit or extra money for it, she was downhearted and decided to do something about it. (Although she sought to be recognized for her work with a promotion or with extra money, the company refused to provide either; so she left.) She discovered she enjoyed the "fitness" aspect of her career and became a consultant to large companies. She taught marketing departments of companies how to develop their fitness programs to help the employees deal with their stress levels. She then followed her passion of fitness and outdoors, and went mountain climbing and hiking all over the world. She fell in love with another country and became an American columnist for a foreign publication based in the United States. After she reached 70 years of age, she developed a plan to continue her teaching of foreign students who enrolled in the university of that foreign country she loved.

Even though both women were limited early on in their careers, *they were not afraid to shift gears and find another career.*

Both of these women served their former university as board members, until the unthinkable happened: Women over 70 were no longer welcome to serve on the board as active members—they became "emeritus" members—even though they had opened up the university to more women. They helped women professors who were caught up in the "publish or perish" syndrome at just the time when these women professors should be having children. The publish syndrome was delayed for these women.

Be sure when you choose you career path that you can work beyond 70 years of age (women do work longer these days). Some careers are geared toward younger women; others have no age limits. Take a look at the career path you have chosen: does this career path allow you to work indefinitely? Can you shift careers?

If you are "older," and are applying for a new position, remember that GenXers and Millennials are different from Boomers and require different ways of communicating. Boomers prefer a telephone call. GenXers and Millennials are much more in tune with emails or texts. Adjust your follow-ups accordingly.

And you will not find so much "gender" bias, as you will find "age" bias. This is a major change in the attitudes of hiring managers, who tend to be Millennials. Adjust your approach accordingly. Many of the Millennials could not find jobs after they graduated in the early 2000s, so they are unlikely to "feel sorry" for you finding yourself out of work. Millennials do not stay in their careers for their lifetime, as you might be inclined to do. Millennials move around more; you should get accustomed to this scenario.

Board Memberships

When you are looking at the next phase of your career, consider a board membership. This might be the step you take before deciding to start your own business or retire.

There are some industries and boards of directors with age limitations; others have no age requirement. Take this factor into consideration when you are choosing a career path—can you use your skills, even after you retire or look at the next phase of your career? Many not-for-profit boards will welcome you, despite your age. From what I have seen, for-profit corporate boards often have an age or experience requirement and usually seem to require board members have a financial background or an area of in-depth expertise.

Several of my friends found board memberships they loved. But it took them some time to find the perfect spot they were looking for. One of my friends was an executive vice president and chief operating officer of a security firm that was sold. She chose not to go with the new company. She joined the National Association of Corporate Directors, took some courses in cyber security, became a board member of the NASD and also became a board member of the Union League of Philadelphia. Later she found other boards that were perfect for her and that provided payment for her time and experience. Another friend had been the chief executive officer of a health system. She also took time to find her "perfect board membership." One of the women had her MBA, the other a PhD. Both were experts in their chosen careers.

Another woman had been in the government; she was asked to become a board member of several corporate boards because of her government experience. When this woman became a board member (in the 90s), it was quite an honor to become a board member without business experience. She reported that she was the only woman on each of the corporate boards. She was listened to, especially when the discussions were about the government; then, her experience was valued. Now, more women are board members and their experience is valued and listened to, and the women are paid for their expertise.

The Forum of Executive Women, based in Philadelphia, helps advertise board membership opportunities (*See* Exhibit 1.1). Most of the opportunities I have seen require bottom-line responsibility. If you want to climb the corporate ladder, look for a career with this experience. Use your economics, accounting, or finance degree to gain your bottom-line experience. Or if you are in a technical industry, become an expert at the technology your industry depends on.

If you are committed to your career, get an advanced degree, like an MBA or a master's degree. An advanced degree is a good path to making more money (but **you have to make sure you negotiate the higher salary; it won't automatically be given to you**). If you want to move into a position that will give you a bottom-line experience, major in economics, accounting, or finance. Don't be afraid of mathematics; keep your eye on an MBA or a master's degree. If you cannot handle math, then major in marketing or management. If you can find a mentor or coach in your organization, you will get the chance to manage profit and loss. That can become the route to the top, as this is a skill that most successful CEOs possess.

Remember that some aspects of careers never change. Check out a career path you would like to pursue; then look at the companies that offer entry level jobs in your chosen career. What are the chances that you can advance in your career? Does the company offer the jobs to promote women in those careers? Do you need continuing education to stay relevant in your chosen career? You don't want to have to leave a company when you hit the glass ceiling because women are blocked off from promotions to top levels. What would you do? What would you be facing? Maybe you should consider leaving that company. If you are content with the glass ceiling, you could stay. *Be happy with the choice you make.*

Exhibit 1.1

Boards of Directors need more women serving on them. Usually boards require a financial background—managing bottom lines. Or sometimes, they are looking for a specific expertise... in this example, a geologist. Whatever field you choose, become an expert in it. Perhaps you will find your niche.

If one of your goals is to become a board member, this is a sample of the questionnaire you might be asked to complete.

Board Member Search Opportunity

Company Description

A diversified mineral public company operating in the United States, primarily central and western states. Their products are used in agriculture (fertilizer input and animal feed), industrial applications, and water for oilfield services. About 500 employees and less than $250 million revenue.

Characteristics Needed
- Accounting expertise appropriate to serve on Audit Committee
- Relevant industry experience in oil and gas, mining, or agriculture
- Relevant scientific background such as a geologist would be a plus but is not expected

Other Information

Compensation—Cash Retainer over $60,000 plus committee fees and Stock Awards

Estimated time required—4 regular board meetings plus committee duties

If you are interested, please submit the following:

1. Cover letter highlighting fit with this specific opportunity
2. Board Bio
3. Board Resume or CV

Please note—our board resource committee will review candidate materials and will pass along those candidates that meet the required criteria. You will be notified on the decision of the committee.

CHAPTER 2

Taking Advantage of Opportunities

Life is a series of opportunities. And most opportunities come to you via other people. As author/humorist Jarod Kintz has said, "It's not who you know that matters—it's who knows you that's important." *It's the people who know you who can help you when you need help, or can introduce you to someone else who can help you.*

Have you ever said, when faced with a problem, "I don't need any help, I can do this on my own." Well, no you can't. Or at least you shouldn't. *Never be too proud to let someone help you, or introduce you to a connection who could help you. Say "yes" to anyone who offers.* No one offers to help unless they really want to assist you. What do you have to lose? You will gain another connection, and you never know if that connection might be just the person to bring you some new opportunity—like a job, when you're in the job market.

In the business world, connections—your network of friends and acquaintances—are important for everyone but doubly important for women; men seem to have an easier time with connections than women. If someone thinks enough of you to want to introduce you to someone else, say "Thank you, I will do it."

Sell Yourself

Take advantage of any opportunity you have to make a new connection, even if it is through a parent or a relative or a friend or anyone who can help you get the introduction. That existing acquaintance can only open the door for you; **you have to sell yourself at the first meeting** with the new connection. But with a good reference from someone who already knows you, the person who's meeting you for the first time will be more inclined to listen to you.

On job interviews, be sure you have ready your two-minute pitch speech that quickly summarizes your talents, your accomplishments and what you can do for that company. Keep working on these two minutes; you never know when you will need them. (As an example, a few years ago, I applied for membership in the Union League of Philadelphia. At the formal interview, the membership committee asked me to *briefly* tell them about my business. How do you summarize 35 years in two minutes? I hadn't expected that particular question, but I had enough experience doing new business pitches that I was able to answer the question coherently.) So, always be prepared to talk about yourself and your talents in two minutes, and keep your response up to date as you progress in your career.

Study the company beforehand, so you know all you can about it. Even if you have little interest in that particular company, go anyway for the interview experience and hope the interviewer is impressed enough with you to give you the name of another company or someone else who could help you. Opportunities abound. Even if you have only the slightest interest, take advantage of it. It will build up your list of connections and references. Women, especially, will notice that good references will serve them really well.

Personal Connections Help

Be alert for opportunities to make a *personal* connection with people you meet. That is a common thread in the careers of several of my college classmates. One of them, an architect named Leslie, was consulting on an architecture project in London. I'll let her tell the story:

> "I was involved in a program to bring together local architects and Prince Charles, and establish a Foundation for Architecture as I had done in Philadelphia. The Prince had... established his own school of architecture. I was in his assistant's office, waiting for a meeting, when I saw behind her desk a very high contrast photograph of the gardens of Villa Lante in central Italy. I commented to her about the image, asking her if it was the Villa Lante. She said, "Yes, how could you tell?" I said, "Oh, I used to teach the history and theory of landscape architecture at the

University of Texas, and this is my absolute favorite renaissance garden and villa." "Really?" she responded. "Have you been there?" "No, I haven't been there, but I'd really like to go." "Well," she said. "It just so happens we're having our summer program there this year, and we need a professor of landscape architecture. Would you be interested?" I replied immediately, "Of course I'd be interested!" I spent several weeks on the faculty of Prince Charles' international program. On the last night, Prince Charles hosted a very small dinner in the villa for the students and faculty, about 25. I was seated next to him."[1]

How's that for making a connection?

Right after graduation, Leslie was going around interviewing for a job—*any* job. Most places wouldn't even let her in the door.

Finally I did get in the door at a major advertising agency. I was sitting in the waiting room and I noticed the boys were being called to go to the left door, and the girls were going to the right door. I went to the receptionist and I said, "Why are the girls going to the right door and the boys are going to the left door?" She said, "That's our executive training program to the left." I asked, "What's to the right?" She said, "That's our secretarial program." I said, "Well I don't want to be a secretary. I want to go in the executive training program." "Oh no, no," she said, "Girls are not allowed."[2]

That was the only time Leslie did not stay for the interview. Leslie ultimately had a very successful career, but moved around a lot. Her success was aided by the fact she had met many important business people when she was in college; she kept in touch with them and didn't hesitate to seek their advice when she moved to another city.

---

[1] Klein, Anne Sceia, *On The Cusp: The Women of Penn '64* (Pine Road Press, 2018), 59–60.

[2] *Id.*, 60–61.

It's All About Contacts and Connections

I found that taking advantage of opportunities and contacts is the story of my life. When I graduated from The Wharton School with a marketing degree, I met with the director of Penn's Women's Placement Service. She was accustomed to placing only teachers and nurses, but did know one woman in the marketing field. Knowing the odds were not on my side, I leaned on the self-reliance my parents and my education had taught me. I contacted this industry woman; she knew another woman who was running an executive search agency. The head of the agency had placed a woman in the public relations department of the regional transit agency. I met with her, and she hired me to work in her department to start off my career. She became a good friend, and after 50 years, remains so.

On one occasion, *not* taking advantage of an opportunity paid off. I went for the interview, then turned down the job because I didn't really want the particular job that was open. Five months later, I received a phone call that the job I really wanted had become available, so I took it. That was an opportunity I could not afford to turn down.

Another classmate, Faye, went to medical school in the 1960s in New York City (she was one of only 12 women in a class of 125) and began her medical career at a major New York City hospital, specializing in radiology. Her story illustrates the importance of making connections:

> ...four radiology residents took me under their wings and mentored me. Little did we know at the time, three of these physicians ultimately would become department chairmen at prestigious medical centers (choose your mentors wisely).[3]

Faye decided to move on from New York City. The connections she had made held her in good stead:

> The Chairman of Radiology at Presbyterian Hospital phoned his very good friend, the Chairman of Radiology at the University of California, San Francisco (UCSF). It turned out one of the

---

[3] *Id.*, 129.

radiology residents had just been drafted and sent to Vietnam. I got the vacant position.[4]

When she arrived, Faye was put in charge of a brand new technology that no one had any experience with: an ultrasound machine. Faye became a self-taught expert in ultrasound and spent the next 17 years practicing and teaching at San Francisco General Hospital (SFGH), the teaching arm of UCSF. Then her connections came through again: one of her SFGH colleagues moved east to Harvard's Brigham & Women's Hospital and recruited Faye to become Director of Education and Training.

After 19 years in Boston, Faye decided to retire, and moved to Washington, DC. Once there, she discovered that both the chairman and vice chairman of Georgetown University Hospital's Radiology Department were former colleagues at San Francisco General.

One thing led to another and for the next six years, I was thrilled to work part-time at GUH.[5]

So, over 42 years, Faye's connections had a major impact on her career.

Switching Career Paths

Another classmate, Neen, built a career on taking advantage of a variety of different opportunities. She had originally wanted to become a doctor. Neen's father was a taxi driver and her mother worked at a local department store, and had started a small business in her home. After her mother's home business failed, Neen—unable to afford medical school—gave up her aspirations to become a physician. She had always enjoyed writing, so she switched her major to English. Her first job was writing and editing young adult book reviews. She realized she had an interest in working with young people, so she pursued a Master's degree in teaching at Harvard. After that, Neen explored several different teaching opportunities: she was

---

[4] *Id.*, 130.
[5] *Id.*, 131.

a volunteer teacher in Israel, a Philadelphia public school teacher and a tutor for Native American children in Utah.

She then returned to Harvard for her PhD. There she met the man who would become her husband a few years later. When she was eight months pregnant, Neen was selected to be head of a small K to 12 coed private school in Manhattan, where she stayed for 14 years. After that, she became chief operating officer of an advocacy and research association at the United Nations. That led to a position on the board of a foundation supporting biomedical research, which in turn led to her being appointed chief executive officer and president of the foundation. When her husband retired and they moved to Florida, Neen became a special advisor to a major medical research institute. Later, she was asked to open a private high school and became its founding Head of School. After that, she became a consultant to various nonprofit organizations and schools.

Neen "retired" at age 72, but couldn't sit still. Leaving her son and husband at home, she joined the Peace Corps and spent 15 months in the South Pacific. After returning, she continued to consult: she was hired to help evaluate the future of a residential juvenile correctional facility in New York State, and the K to 12 education system in the United Arab Emirates.

Neen's amazing career was defined by opportunities, connections, and contacts:

> I have been the beneficiary of good people. Throughout the years, I have been delighted to help many young people secure employment or school admission by calling on my large network of contacts in the various fields I have nurtured. I have never forgotten the successful individuals in my life who were generous and helpful when I needed someone to "open a door" to give me access when I had none, and to encourage me to "reach for the brass ring." I remain grateful to the men and women who gave me a chance to prove myself, who respected me for my achievements and valued my qualities.[6]

---

[6] *Id.*, 116.

Cultivate Your Opportunities

Another woman, Ilene, became a teacher after graduation. But she never wanted to teach. After a few years, she moved to New York City. She applied for a job at McKinsey & Company, a major consulting firm, and tested very well—she received the highest grade in statistics. She got the job. Ilene was extremely talented and worked hard to rise through the ranks in what traditionally had been a very male-oriented profession. Nevertheless, she *says it's important, especially for women, to cultivate mentors in a business world*:

> I owe my entire career to the men in the McKinsey public practice group. They bent over backward to be my sponsors and protectors from their colleagues who opposed women in consulting roles. With their sponsorship, I was promoted to the consulting staff in 1974. Once I became a consultant, I was treated with more respect.[7]

Eventually Ilene wanted to move on, and her contacts helped her.

> My area of interest was executive resources, and I became head of worldwide human resources at Revlon, when it was a Fortune 200 company. Abby Rudolph, a man who was at McKinsey, had moved on to Revlon. Marvin Bower, "the father of the consulting profession," told Rudolph to hire me, since he knew I was interested in moving on. Rudolph did hire me and became my next protector.[8]

Ilene later moved on to Estee Lauder and subsequently became a deputy assistant secretary at the federal Department of Housing and Urban Development. A couple of years later, a friend she had met at McKinsey recruited her to Ashoka, a social sector organization that supports entrepreneurs. She stayed there for 15 years, then moved back to New

---

[7] *Id.*, 137.

[8] *Id.*, 138.

York and founded a human resources consulting practice at one of the nation's largest full service advisory and accounting firms. Even after retirement, she continues to consult to small companies and nonprofits, including Carnegie Hall and the Metropolitan Opera in New York City.

Opportunities and contacts clearly were important in her career. And Ilene says she disagrees strongly with Sheryl Sandberg, COO of Facebook and author of *Lean In*. Ilene feels that Ms. Sandberg demeaned women who had to "fit in" in order to survive.

> I find that lacking in understanding of the challenges of working in male-dominated companies in the early days. I did everything I possibly could to assist other women. Yes, we did have to "fit in." If we hadn't helped each other and fit in, Sheryl Sandberg might not have a job today.[9]

Thankfully, the world has opened up to women. We cannot stop "going for it." Taking advantage of opportunities and connections is as important today as it ever was.

---

[9] *Id.*, 139.

CHAPTER 3

Making the Choice: A Family or a Career? Can You Have Both?

This is a subject most women do not or will not discuss. Among women, why not talk about it? The subject is taboo; I believe that most women will not discuss their decision for fear their decision may be passed along to their boss. (Horrible—why can't we trust one another? Do we still have the innate fear of one another?)

From almost the day I started my business, I kept looking for someone who eventually would be able to take it over. My very first employee was a talented young woman who started with me as an intern and rose to become a vice president. She was bright and motivated, and showed potential to run the business one day. She had baby number one very early on, when the business was still in my house. It was no problem; either her husband or her aunt would look after the baby while she was at work. Most times, she would bring the baby into work and let her sleep in our bedroom. And we were flexible about her hours, so everything worked out fine.

A few years later, baby number two was on its way. The firm had grown to several employees by that point. Knowing she would need time off for baby number two, we gave her 12 weeks of maternity leave and hired a freelancer to fill in for her. When she came back to her job after her leave, everything had changed. The freelancer (an experienced senior practitioner) had made many improvements, and the firm had even moved its offices to a new location. Between the totally new environment, the work of taking care of two children (her husband was busy with his own career and was not able to become a Mr. Mom), plus the issue of the cost of childcare, she wasn't able to do it all. So she resigned after a couple of weeks. (By the way, my original instinct that she would have been able to eventually take over my business was correct. Many years later, when her children were able to care for themselves, she started her own business and was very successful.)

Later on, we collaborated with other women of childbearing age in our firm to develop a formal maternity leave policy that would not cut off a woman entirely from the office for 12 weeks. We found a way to allow the woman, after two weeks, to call in once a week for updates. (We would also copy her on relevant emails.) Gradually we increased the number of calls per week, then had her come into the office once a week, then twice, and so on until she was ready to come back full time.

Numerous studies show that many women don't return to the workforce after childbirth. A British study found that only 29 percent of first-time mothers, and less than 20 percent of all new mothers, return to full-time work in the first three years after maternity leave.[1] A University of Michigan study found that "More than 40 percent of women with full-time jobs in science leave the sector or go part time after having their first child."[2] A Princeton University study found that "women are more likely to leave after their first child regardless of how many more times they give birth. However, women who ultimately have more children are always more likely to leave, even prior to having these later births."[3]

Get the Advanced Degree

Women also tend to forego advanced education when they have to manage both a career and a family. (Get the advanced degree while you can.) Even if your company is willing to help you manage your financial investment in your education, but has a time requirement for you to stay in

---

[1] Findings by researchers at the Universities of Bristol and Essex as reported at https://workplaceinsight.net/women-less-likely-to-progress-at-work-than-their-male-counterparts-following-childbirth/

[2] https://nature.com/articles/d41586-019-00611-1

[3] https://princeton.edu/news/2018/10/22/women-most-likely-leave-labor-force-after-first-child-not-later-births

your job once your education is complete, this path is still difficult for women.

Studies too numerous to mention show that men tend to make more money than women, the Lilly Ledbetter and other laws notwithstanding (*see* page 42). That's why, in many families where the economics allow it, the wife stays home to raise the children and the father works to support them (although this was much more prevalent in the mid-twentieth century before dual incomes became almost a necessity for many couples). Much of that is due simply to biology. Women are the mothers; that is who they are. Women have the children, and the urge to be a mother is not a small factor, especially as age advances and the biological clock keeps ticking.

> The best chance for women to "have it all" comes if they marry early and have their children in their 20s. Once a woman reaches her 30s and beyond, her career is pretty much set, and it becomes more difficult to leave the workforce to have a family.

The days are past when a company was so bold as to tell me that if I got pregnant, I would lose my spot in line for a promotion, that I would be competing against other men and women who did not take off time to have a baby. Nevertheless, studies do show that women returning to the workforce are at a disadvantage, even more so the longer they have been out. The growth of paternity leave has helped soften the impact, but the reality persists.

Infertility/Adoption

Many women who try to get pregnant simply cannot. They may try to see a fertility doctor, take different drugs, and begin what could be a long process. Some couples decide to adopt a child. Fortunately, the adoption rules have changed since the 1980s when you could not adopt if you were over 40 years old. That was not the only barrier to adoption.

I remember a young staff member who tried to get pregnant for several years. When she couldn't, she and her husband decided to adopt a child. This woman was a vice president and made a decent salary—her job was the very reason why she and her husband were financially able to adopt. But it was the 1990s; one adoption agency told her she would have to take six months off to be with a child. Another agency told her she would have to stay at home for a full year. She obviously went with the agency that told her she would have to take off only six months. She and her husband adopted a boy from Asia. The staff member did not return to our firm but later worked on a temporary, part-time basis for a major corporation. She eventually worked her way into a full-time position and did very well.

Adoption is certainly an option for women, couples, or partners. One friend, a single professional woman, adopted a child from Kazakhstan; the adopted child is now 12 years old, and she is adorable. Another couple (in their 50s) adopted a grown son from Russia. The east coast couple moved to California because the father's job was transferred. They have since moved back to the east coast, because they were worried the adopted son was embracing a California surfer attitude and was becoming too lax in his ambition. At last word, the adopted son was doing fine.

There can also be pitfalls to an adoption. Many years ago, a friend adopted a young girl but later told me that she had to give her up. There must have been some mental health issues, because the child threatened to kill my friend, a high-level commercial lending officer at a bank. There is a great deal more medical and psychological testing these days, so I think this scenario would be less likely to repeat today.

One friend, when she was younger, had her eggs frozen and, much later, found a sperm donor. When she was in her 40s, she decided it was time to have her daughter (who is adorable, by the way). My friend had a great career going for her, and moved around to advance to her vice presidency. Personally, I think this is a high-risk move to make, but for my friend, it worked out well.

I got married when I was 34. My father did all he could to encourage me to try to have a family as soon as possible. He even agreed to pay my mortgage. But then my husband went to law school, delaying my decision even further. At 39 years of age (yes, I thought I was a "super-woman"), and after wasting a year with a doctor who never even taught me how to take my temperature properly, I finally decided to make a change to a fertility doctor with a good track record. After four years of trying (x-rays, drugs, injections), I still had no luck. I would have gone on indefinitely because the urge to have a child becomes paramount. But we need to know when it is time to quit trying to get pregnant. At the urging of my parents and my husband, I finally quit seeing the fertility doctor when I was 44. Fortunately, my husband understood, and told me that we should "play the hand we were dealt."

Life Can Be Tough

We understand that if we choose the motherhood route, we have to make some serious decisions, perhaps to give up our career unless we have a husband who can afford the expense of daycare, an *au pair*, or a nanny. We like to think the world has changed but, biologically and culturally, the woman still assumes most of the burden of caring for the child.

There are some women fortunate enough to marry men who are willing and able to step into the role of "Mr. Mom" and take over a significant part of the child-raising burden. Regrettably, too many men still think that it is the mother's job to stay home to care for the children and look after the home. Fortunately, this attitude is changing too, as many men now understand that "staying home" is work as well, and that stay-at-home moms need a "break" from their routine at the end of a long day. *The division of household tasks is an important discussion to have BEFORE you decide to marry, but even more so before you make the decision to have a family.*

Several of my classmates met their future husbands in college. They married early and had their children early. Some of them opted to stay at home while their children were young; others chose to work immediately. One of my classmates said she loved being married in the 1960s, because a husband's role and that of his wife were more clearly defined. I don't know if I agree with her assessment, but it worked for my classmate, and that is what counts. **Be sure you understand your role, today, when life and times are very different.**

Balance Your Life

Classmates who never married rose to the top of their careers. One classmate became a senior vice president of a Philadelphia-area bank. Another classmate, who headed the human resources department at a major corporation, told me about a colleague of hers who mentioned she wanted to become a partner in her firm. My friend counseled her and said, "You should devote your life to this goal." The woman eventually did become a partner.

Times don't change all that much. Women have to be as serious about their careers as men are. **It is no easy task to balance both a career and a family**; usually, something has to be given up, unless you are fortunate enough to be like another classmate of mine. She is a physician who married another physician. Her parents moved 2000 miles to be near their daughter and raise their granddaughter. Not everyone is this fortunate.

Women who have made it to the very top—like Mary Barra (CEO of General Motors), Ellen Kullman (former CEO of DuPont) and Indra Nooyi (former CEO of PepsiCo)—make a great deal of money, but they have also had to work extremely hard. Many don't make it to the top until later in life (in their 50s and 60s).

Children or Not?

There are many elements that will influence your decision, among them are your desire to advance in your career and your age. Women do have a biological clock. Have your children while you can. You may never have "enough" money to have a family, so evaluate and prioritize your risk factors (*see* Exhibit 3.1).

The decision becomes easier (and yet more difficult to make) if both the wife and husband have well-paying jobs, sometimes even in the same company. The days are long gone when two attorneys or two consultants, or so on, could not work in the same firm once they got married. It used to be that the person with the best salary, or future prospects, stayed while the other spouse found another firm. This was a difficult choice for women to make. Thankfully, women generally no longer have to make this choice. *The choice to be made is whether or not to have a family.* Many couples decide their life is more important than the family, but it is a choice to be made.

Exhibit 3.1 Risks and priorities to assess if you want to have a family

- How old are you?
- How healthy are you?
- Can you live on one income?
- How important is your career to you?
- How often does your job require travel?
- Can you easily work from home?
- Can you take time off when you wish?
- Do women advance in their careers in your organization if they have children?
- Do you receive compensatory time?
- Does your company value an advanced degree?
- Do you have an advanced degree?
- Can you set aside enough time to study for an advanced degree?
- Have you and your spouse/partner discussed having a family?
- How supportive is your spouse/partner of having a family?
- Are there any other concerns or questions you have?

CHAPTER 4

Networking and Promoting Your Talent

I am considered an introverted/extrovert on the Myers-Briggs personality test. (I don't know if I really was introverted because I didn't want the job I was tested for. I was persuaded to take the test by the man who wanted to hire me. But I did answer the questions honestly).

As someone who is an introvert at heart, I knew I had to change to be a success in my career. How did I do that? I had good role models in my parents and my grandmothers (my grandfathers passed away before I was born). I also am an only child, so if I wanted to have friends, I had to learn to be more outgoing.

I also learned to be nice to the men in my classes at Wharton; I became cordial as though I were a sibling. This was the only way I was able to survive in an environment where there were so many men and only a handful of women. My time in college was difficult. I found that I had to work harder than I expected, and I was not exposed to networking opportunities. In fact, there were no outside speakers except men, so I assumed that was the way it was. It never occurred to me that professional women in business were few and far between. I learned later in life that I would have to deal with it. I did pretty well, not realizing what was going on, but I coped with it and sometimes got very angry. (I had been angry at one particular man at a chemical company we pitched who did not hire our firm. I thought it was because we were a woman-owned business. But I was very wrong. I learned recently that he *never* hired outside resources. The lesson I learned is that you must look into hiring practices beforehand.)

I am comfortable being alone, but as I've gotten older, I realize that family and friends are important. The problem I face now is that my friends are scattered worldwide, so keeping in touch is a challenge. I'm already pretty adept at email, having used it in the office for many years. But now I am teaching myself some new skills: I have become pretty comfortable with video chatting using Skype, and I'm learning to use Zoom. (I tell my husband he will have to outlive me, because each time I'm confused, he is there to help me out.) Technology is changing all the time and it's hard for me to keep up. You must do your best to keep up with technological changes.

Networking Is Essential

In business, though, I found networking to be essential. Especially as the owner of a business, networking was a vital part of identifying and cultivating potential new clients to build my business. Every client we won was through an introduction from someone we had met. Every job I had in the corporate world came via a friend or contact.

There are networking opportunities everywhere—at work, at social events, even at family and friends' events. Consider your high school or college alumni associations and chambers of commerce.

Start by telling your family what you do. I don't think I was ever fully successful in explaining my business to my parents, but I tried. You never know who your parents know. My parents did their best to assist me. My father was a very good dentist, and he built his practice through word-of-mouth. But after he exhausted his network helping me get accepted at college, neither he nor my mother could help me anymore; I was on my own.

I found that business networking became a refinement of my social skills. My business friends say I am the ultimate networker! *I became a "connector,"* introducing people I met to other people I knew. Even recently, I introduced one of my graduate school classmates—an investor in biopharmaceutical companies—to someone I had met who has a background in pharmaceuticals. I received an email from my classmate telling me that he and the person I introduced him to have become great friends, and are working together on developing a therapeutic medication.

I also found that you have to get out of your office to network. In-person networking skills are crucial, so if you are shy, get over it. Forget "sending an email" or "making a phone call" until later in the process. Building a worthwhile network involves meeting people in person.

Networking 101

When you are going to a meeting or an event, wear your company's name tag. Throw out the one you are given by the organization hosting the event—the one that has the organization's name in large type and your name in small type. Think about how many times you've seen that kind of name tag and have not been able to read the person's name. Be smart—make your own name tag, with the company's name smaller (but still readable) and your name larger. If you forget to bring your own name tag to a meeting, use a blank one at the sign-in desk and write your first name very large. Then, as you meet people and start conversing, you can hand them your business card, which will provide further information.

Ladies, if you don't absolutely need a handbag or briefcase during the meeting, leave it in the trunk of your car or check it at the coat check (just don't have a lot of cash in your handbag). Before the meeting starts, go to the ladies room to comb your hair and put on powder and lipstick. Then you can check your handbag, leaving your hands free.

When you go to that meeting or event, be sure to take along a large stack of your business cards. Put them in your pocket, and don't be afraid to hand one out when you meet a new person. Be sure the suit you wear (or dress or pant suit) has deep pockets to hold your cards and a facial tissue. Look as professional as you can. Wear comfortable shoes. Now, you are ready to network at your meeting or event.

Here are some other tips: When you walk into a room, look around. Do you see someone you know talking with someone you don't know? Say hello to the person whom you know, and introduce yourself to the person you don't know, and don't be afraid to join the conversation. By doing that, you've just added one more person to your network.

Don't assume someone you know or have met before will remember your name or recognize you out of context. **ALWAYS say your name.** (How many times do you say to yourself, "I recognize that person but I do not remember his/her name.") Conversely, if someone comes up to you and says "Hi" but doesn't give his or her name, you can always say something like, "I'm blanking on your name. I know you but I just can't remember your name." The response will help you network… and help you remember names!

If there is a list of people attending the event, take a few minutes to review the list in advance. Once in the meeting, find someone you know and start a conversation, just to break the ice and get yourself in "networking mode." That will help you build confidence to start conversations with people you don't yet know.

Also, scan the list to see if there are people you would like to know and make a list of everyone who could be a potential prospect. Make a point to meet at least one or two of them, and say hello. Introduce yourself. You never know who might know someone who knows someone else in need of your services. If you can do that at every meeting or event, consider your networking a success.

Remember to Follow-Up

Write or email your new contacts that evening or the next day. If the person is "young," you can send an email; if the person is "older," a handwritten note might be more appropriate. Writing notes by hand is a dying art, and an older person will appreciate a handwritten note much more than an email. (You can always send both.) A handwritten note is so out-of-the-ordinary these days that the person you're writing to is much more likely to remember who you are.

Don't assume that everyone in the room knows everyone else. Walk up to someone who is standing alone and say hello. If you don't know anyone else in the room, saying so is a good conversation starter. (This is not a negative for you.) If the other person does know someone else, they might introduce you to someone new. If not, you and your new friend might want to walk around the room to introduce yourselves to more people. Not only will you make a new friend, but you may wind up meeting several others.

You can also meet people at the bar or in the buffet line. Strike up a conversation, even if it's just something about the food looking good, or that the bar has a good selection of wines, or whatever. This is another good opportunity to meet others.

When attending a lunch or dinner meeting where the other people at my table are strangers, I always say, "I refuse to sit at a table without knowing everyone." Then, I tell them my name and my company.

If someone asks you what you do or what your company does, give them your 30-second "elevator speech."

> An elevator speech is a very short summary of who you are and what you do that can be completed in the span of a short elevator ride.

An example of an elevator speech for our firm might have been: "We are an internationally recognized public relations firm with expertise in crisis and issues preparedness and response. We are also experts in community relations, environmental communications, and spokesperson training."

Then ask them what they do. **Connections are what networking is all about**. Listen carefully to what the other person is saying. If you have a connection, mention who or what the connection is: maybe it's business, maybe it's sports, maybe it's mutual friends or having gone to the same college. It can be anything that links you to that other person. If there is a connection, write the person an email the next day to reinforce the connection. If the conversation is going well, you'll definitely want to hand that person a business card, if you have not already done so.

It has become customary to hand out a business card to everyone at the table. Remember, it's how you do it that matters. Don't be obnoxious; if someone doesn't want your card, then move on to the next person. Think about the times you've taken a business a card you didn't really want; how did you react? Hand out your card graciously, and with a smile, whether or not the prospect is a good connection for you. On the outside chance you might connect with the one person who is interested in what you do, then the networking will be worth your time.

Other Things You Can Do to Make Connections

Make a list of everyone you know who could be a referral source for you. Then establish a regular program of contacting them. The best way to really get to know your contacts is through entertaining at a breakfast, lunch, dinner, or a sporting or theatrical event—anything "social." Entertain your good existing referral sources. Send them birthday and holiday cards.

Tell them what you do. But NEVER directly ask your contact for business. Rather, ask them to keep you in mind and mention your name if they hear of someone looking for the services you provide. Send them a "please refer us" letter.

> The "please refer us" letter is a letter that outlines your company's or your services, and asks the person to whom you send it to pass the letter along if they know of another company that could use your services. (Your objective is, hopefully, to make the "short list" of companies or people being considered for a job.)

If you have a company or personal newsletter, put your referral sources and other networking contacts on the list to receive news about you or your company. You don't have to issue a newsletter monthly, but be consistent. Our firm sent out a newsletter three times a year for more than 25 years; many people thought it came out monthly. The four-page newsletter was a quick read and, over time, we built the mailing list to about 3,500 recipients.

Our firm received many awards over the years, so the most recent award was usually the main story on the front page. Also, on the front page was an editorial that I wrote—mostly about a current issue or a service I wanted to promote. Inside, we listed staff achievements and client news. On page three, we wrote a longer feature, "Spotlight on a Client." Page four was used for overflow—usually my editorial—along with the address area and the postage indicia.

We felt the newsletter was very effective in keeping our name in front of people. Often, when we ran into people whose names were on our mailing list, they would comment that they enjoyed the newsletter very much. It was not unusual, shortly after the newsletter was mailed out, for us to receive inquiries about our services. The newsletter served an important purpose: it reminded people who we were and what we did, and kept our name at the top of their mind.

One of the best ways to make contacts is to join a professional or business organization. Then, work hard to get known in that organization. Become an officer or work on a committee. Try to link up with another company or individual in the same field as you but who offers something different from what you offer.

I recall I teamed up with an environmental engineering firm whose work dovetailed with the work we were doing in environmental communications. We were able to do several joint programs together, which helped my firm get known beyond the confines of my own professional organizations.

If there is an organization you have heard about but are unsure of joining, then go for a couple of meetings by paying the "guest" rate so you can see who the members are. If there appears to be no opportunity, then don't bother wasting your time joining. But if you think there is an opportunity, then join the organization and get known.

Other Organizations to Join

You can also join a charitable organization if you believe in the organization and its mission. Networking is not the main objective here, but you never know. And do join an international organization where you can meet people from around the world. Giving a lecture in another country is a great way to enhance your reputation at home; plus, it's a great way to see the world. I accomplished this networking by joining a group called Pinnacle Worldwide, an international network of independent public relations firms. Our firm became well known, so we were invited to join Pinnacle. (You can find international organizations by doing an internet search and entering the name "reference—international organizations." An internet search should assist you, but you can always ask your librarian to help you find a directory in your field.)

My husband became an officer of Pinnacle and eventually became the president and later chairman. I became the membership chair and was able to reach out and meet people all over the world. It's amazing who your existing members know in other countries! I made friends worldwide.

Promote Your Talent

Use every opportunity you have to promote your talent (*see* Exhibit 4.1). When you thank your team, be sure to mention it is YOUR team. When you have a success, let as many people as possible know about it. *Give speeches or write articles or case studies about what you do.*

Exhibit 4.1 Promoting yourself through articles and speeches

Your own reading should give you an idea of the types of stories editors are interested in knowing about.

Contact the editor of your regional publication and let him/her know of your interest in writing or being interviewed.

If there are national publications, contact the editor and let him/her know you are available to be interviewed on a subject of national interest.

If you are willing to be a resource to the press, be sure they have your home or cell phone number so you can be reached at a moments' notice, especially when the editor or reporter is writing the story.

If you are not shy about speaking your thoughts, you can also let a radio or TV producer know about your interests on various subjects. Remember that the media love conflict and controversy. If you are comfortable being controversial, then "go for it!"

If you prefer to keep your comments noncontroversial, then you can become an expert in your field—like a computer expert or a legal expert on engineering or accounting. (I was told that an attorney was hired by her firm because she "appeared" regularly in *The Legal Intelligencer*, a Philadelphia legal newspaper.)

If you have an area of expertise (mine was crisis communication), write a case study about the subject. (I wrote/gave speeches about "Crises of a Generation" where I recounted the major and well-known crises that had taken place over 30 years.)

Of course, get to know someone at your area's all-news radio station. I was called regularly about crises situations. I was careful NEVER to say anything bad about a client or person—you have to know the laws that regulate your area of expertise. I used the HIPAA law to explain why President Ford was able to go back to his hotel after his stroke in 2000.

Although I didn't say anything bad about anyone, the media still called me; they knew about my expertise in crisis communications. Even though I was located in New Jersey, I received a call from a California radio station asking me to comment on Martha Stewart and the insider trading charges against her. Another time, I was quoted in an article about the Ford vs. Firestone tire controversy. You can do this too.

Get to know the editors of publications that reach your audience, or bloggers that write about an area of your expertise. A good case study is worth the time you put in to write about it.

Try to meet the CEOs of companies who belong to an organization where you are a member. Everyone I ever met at our regional Chamber of Commerce was a leader in his or her company. Introduce yourself to people, especially if you have heard of them or heard them make a speech. Find an excuse to talk with them further about a subject of interest to them—NOT you. After a while, you will meet many people who might become business colleagues. You'll be invited to join other organizations. The regional vice president of a national organization once asked me to join HIS board because of MY connections. That's a good thing.

One final tip: If one of your referral sources asks for you to do a favor, **never** say no. *Networking is a two-way street.* You have been asking people to keep you in mind. The least you can do is return the favor. If you are unable to do it personally, offer to find someone else to help out.

Chapter 4 Summary

Networking is Making Connections and Refining Your Social Skills

- Start with your family and friends
- Leave your office to network
- Word-of-mouth marketing
- Go to a meeting or an event:
  - Bring your name tag with you—in large print
  - Bring an adequate supply of business cards that should be designed to have your name and your phone number readable. (Think of how many times you could not read a business card given to you.) You are better off to stay with a white or light-colored card and a dark ink that is readable.
- Look around when you walk into a room. Do you see someone you know?
- Say hello to someone you don't know
- Reinforce your name—say it to the new person or someone you might already know
- Say something nice to the person in front of you or behind you in the buffet line or at the bar
- Review the guest list if it is available
- Distribute your cards to everyone at your table

Other Networking Opportunities

- Make a list of everyone you know who could be a referral source
- Establish a regular contact program of breakfast or lunch
- Take the contact to a sporting event or a social event
- Send a personal or company newsletter
- Join a professional or business organization—get on a committee; get in line to become an officer
- Join an international organization
- Give a speech
- Write an article
- Do a favor, if you can

CHAPTER 5

Gender Inequality and Bias

Despite everything you may have heard about progress toward gender equality in pay, women still generally earn less than men. According to an ongoing study by Payscale.com, looking at the median earnings of women versus men, women in 2020 make only 81 cents for every dollar men make.[1] That's a seven cent improvement since 2015, but clearly women still have a way to go.

As a woman entering the work force, or if you are moving up in your career, **you are very likely to encounter pay discrepancies and biases during your career, especially if you enter a predominantly male field** like construction or transportation. I was so naïve when I entered the business world in the mid-1960s. I did not realize there were barriers, so I just forged ahead, ignoring what should have been my wake-up call: a lower salary, tests that seemed irrelevant, and not being hired for a job I was clearly qualified to do. I never have tested well. I recall these tests were for intelligence and personality. Men took the tests as well, but in looking back, I don't think I was ever told how I did, who graded the tests, and who made the hiring decision. I remember that after one particularly frustrating experience with a test early in my career, I never wanted to take any more tests and I never did. You can avoid tests by having good referral sources and an excellent track record.

---

[1] https://payscale.com/data/gender-pay-gap. That is the "raw" gender pay gap, which does not control for various compensable factors. It is the number you generally hear reported on in the news media. However, Payscale.com also reports that when the gender pay gap analysis is controlled for job title, years of experience, industry, location, and other compensable factors, women make 98 cents for every dollar men make. But that number has increased only one cent since 2015. *Id.*

Women are much more aware of biases today, and are careful to choose their words wisely when they apply for a career position. While women don't have to and shouldn't act like men, they are careful never to discuss the prospect of having children in their future. But there still are men smart enough to find a way to discover if the woman is bent on having children.[2] In a 2019 Forbes article,[3] Victoria Sprott, Staff Development and Talent Director of Robert Half UK (United Kingdom—England), suggested a response like, "[B]efore I answer I would like to understand how that question is relevant to my ability to perform in this role." One of my classmates passed along another piece of advice she received from a business colleague: when you are asked, "How can you manage an early business meeting or travel when you have children?" Turn the question around and say, "I'd handle it the same way you do/would do if/when you have children." This often will throw the interviewer off, and he will move on to the next question. The idea is to gently but firmly signal to the interviewer that the topic should be out of bounds.

Some men don't seem to consider how seriously women approach their careers, even with children. Many hard-working women have amazing track records and definitely are worthy of a promotion or increased salary. The old saw, that women have to work twice as hard to be seen half as good as men, has a lot of truth to it.

Trends Are Improving

The trend is improving when it comes to hiring, promoting, and paying women. A notable example is the Lilly Ledbetter Fair Pay Act of 2009. It is changing the legal landscape when it comes to pay discrimination against women.

---

[2] "The Equality and Human Rights Commission (EHRC) surveyed 1,106 senior decision makers on behalf of YouGov (who commissioned the research) in 2018 and found that a third (36 percent) of private sector employers think it's OK to ask prospective female employees about their plans for children in the future. Almost half of these employers (46 Percent) also believe it is reasonable to ask women if they have young children during interviews too." https://forbes.com/sites/biancabarratt/2019/01/24/what-to-do-if-youre-asked-about-kids-in-an-interview/#247bc06f6334

[3] Id.

Federal law has given persons who have been discriminated against in pay due to discrimination (whether based on age, religion, national origin, race, sex, or disability) 180 days in which to file a claim against their employer. But a 2007 Supreme Court decision had ruled that the 180-day period began 180 days after the *first* paycheck that manifested discriminatory pay. But because many women don't find out for years that they've been discriminated against, Congress passed the Fair Pay Act to specify that the 180 days begins to run anew with *every* paycheck that reflects the discrimination in pay. *Nevertheless, if you find out you are being paid less than a man with a comparable job, speak up as soon as you can.* Tell the Human Resources director if your boss appears not to understand your situation.

Typically, women don't negotiate as well as they should; that may be one reason why women's pay is less than men's. While the legal environment is getting better, it is very hard for most women to fight biology. Younger women simply don't work as long at building their careers; often they choose to take a break to have children. Some women who are intent on building a career, or who must work to help support their family, return to work almost immediately. But many wait until their children are older and can more readily care for themselves. Upon returning to the job market, these women usually find they have lost ground in terms of position and pay. They are also at a disadvantage because, for the most part, it is the wives who still do the chauffeuring to dance or soccer practice. These disruptions make it easy for the people responsible for the raises or promotions to favor someone who has more education or more experience and who didn't interrupt her career for children.

Many women with children choose "soft" staff positions in human resources and communications for their flexibility. Financial positions are different: you need to love math or data processing and be willing to handle stress. But is this the career you want to have with children? Maybe yes, but maybe no.

Women Supporting Women

Even women who "make it" can be a problem. During my generation, women who had advanced to higher levels often blocked other women from advancing as well. This type of woman was called a "queen bee."

They did not help us, and often were openly hostile, because they felt they had worked so hard to get where they were that they saw other women as a threat. We could not count on them.

This attitude has changed today, because *women know they must look out for and support other women.* Over the years, women have learned to care about other women, not view them as enemies. Younger women often step in to support us.

One of my jobs in the 1960s was at an architectural firm, and my boss hired an older woman to work for him. She refused to help me. I remember well her condescending words: "I don't work for little girls." I was 26 years old and I was so angry. A younger woman—under 20 years old—said she would assist me when her work was finished. Two wonderful young men also offered to assist me on a project I was assigned. Working together with these three individuals, I managed to make it through a year of "hell." Thankfully, one partner and his father (the remaining name partner of the firm) were much more welcoming to women and treated me well. But none of the other partners seemed particularly upset to lose me when I resigned.

Do Corporate Cultures Demoralize Women?

What's worse is that many corporate cultures demoralize women and crush their ambitions to make it to the C-Suite. A Bain & Company survey[4] asked a mix of men and women two questions: "Do you aspire to top management within a large company?" and "Do you have the confidence you can reach top management?" As reported in Harvard Business Review, the survey found that:

> Women with two years or less of work experience slightly led men in ambition. But for women who had more than two years on the job, aspiration and confidence plummeted 60% and nearly 50%, respectively. These declines came independent of marriage and motherhood status, and compared with much smaller changes for men, who experienced only a 10% dip in confidence."[5]

---

[4] https://bain.com/insights/everyday-moments-of-truth
[5] https://hbr.org/2015/05/companies-drain-womens-ambition-after-only-2-year

Why these results? It appears corporations tend to support and celebrate men much more than women:

> To start, the majority of leaders celebrated in a corporate newsletter or an offsite meeting tend to consist of men hailed for pulling all-nighters or for networking their way through the golf course to land the big account. If corporate recognition and rewards focus on those behaviors, women feel less able, let alone motivated to try, to make it to the top.[6]

Clearly, it takes a lot of fortitude and sacrifice to make it to the very top. Is it worth it? Only you can decide how much time and effort you want to invest in your career.

Do Attitudes Change?

The *#MeToo* and *#TimesUp* movements have generally improved men's behavior toward women in the workplace (or at least prompted them to keep their attitudes to themselves). But as women, we should always remember (as much as we hate to admit it) that "boys will be boys." It is counterproductive for women to wear provocative clothing, like short skirts and low-cut blouses. Strive always to look professional. Don't give a man any excuse to make an unwanted approach.

The stories about sexual harassment are still rampant; yet most women still never say a word about it. While interviewing for my book, *On the Cusp: The Women of Penn '64*, I asked my Penn classmates the question, "Were you ever sexually harassed?" Almost uniformly, their individual responses were, "Yes. But I just shut it down." How did they do it? They didn't say. But the way to do it today is easier than you think, starting with your being focused on doing your job… and doing it well. Let the man know you don't have time for unwanted advances, and go back to work. Other times, you may just have to say something directly to his face, like "Are you crazy? Haven't you heard of the scandals and that

---

[6] *Id.*

charges were filed against people like Harvey Weinstein or Matt Lauer?" If the harassment continues, then you may have no choice but to report the behavior to human resources. Be careful not to alienate the other men on your team. It's better if you can say something yourself to get the man to back off (*see* Exhibit 5.1). But please, ladies, don't cry at work, unless you are *extremely* offended by the unwanted advance, or a friend or relative has been given a life-threatening diagnosis or someone close to you has died.

Given my age, I've seen a lot. Some men don't change. Hold your ground if a man comes on to you and you don't appreciate his advances. It's much easier today for men to assume all women are sex objects. *Television and movies nowadays often give the impression that sex on demand is acceptable. It's NOT okay, no matter how you look at it.*

And if you do think about succumbing to a man's advances and think no one in the workplace will find out about it, think again. Men talk. Men brag. It's so easy for you to get a bad reputation as an easy mark in your company. I heard a great saying from a terrific guy who hired me for

Exhibit 5.1 *Ways to shut down unwanted advances*

- I have a boyfriend (and I will tell him what happened).
- I am engaged to marry (and I will tell him what happened).
- I'm married (and I will tell my husband what happened).
- I am working.
- I am pursuing a career.
- Do you want to be a Harvey Weinstein, Roger Ailes or Matt Lauer? (#MeToo #TimesUp)
- I will report you to HR (or any suitable representative for women's issues).

If you are pushed into a corner
- Use your knee to kick the man in the groin—it will paralyze him with pain.
- Tell a friend or a parent.
- Report the incident to Human Resources of a Diversity Manager IN WRITING.

my last corporate job before I started my own business. He told me men tell each other, "Don't get your honey where you make your money." And in the movie "Moonstruck," Olympia Dukakis' character, Rose, watches a college professor get dumped by a student he had been dating. Rose's advice to him: "Don't s**t where you eat." Good advice always. Unfortunately, not all men heed the advice. Just don't be one of those women who "sleep their way to the top." You can be sure most of the men in the company will know how the promotions came about.

Finding Mr. Right in the Office

That is not to say that if a man flirts innocently with you, you can't flirt back. Otherwise, you might never meet Mr. Right. Many marriages get started in the workplace.

I have only a theory—and it's simply Anne's theory—that when the economy is good, men don't care if there are women in their department, as long as they work hard and make the boss look good. When the economy is on the downturn, men feel threatened (like the "queen bee" I mentioned earlier) that the women will take their jobs. And when that happens, then men are motivated to discriminate against women.

Despite lingering instances of discrimination, *remember you can take advantage of many opportunities that I didn't even have.* You can choose any career path—something that will make you happy—just in case Mr. Right doesn't come along. Work hard at your career. Become known in your firm as a woman with a mission—someone who is worthy of a promotion and increased salary.

Money Isn't the Only Thing

Fight for the salary you deserve, but remember money isn't the only thing in life. Find a position where there is a good work/life balance or decent intangible benefits, like being able to leave early on occasion. If you want to climb the corporate ladder, then be sure it's the ladder you actually want. Look at the men around you… are you willing to make the sacrifices the men have made in trying to make it to the top? If you are, then go for it.

Keep your head above water. If you work hard, your efforts should be recognized by someone higher up than your boss. Give it a couple of years; if nothing changes, then it might be time to move on. Always do the best job you can, and when you think it's hopeless, then the time has come to make the move. *Remember, often the best way to get a large boost in salary is to move to another job at another company.* Many in my generation stayed in the same job or same company for their entire careers. Young people today tend to move around multiple times, so it's no longer a matter of being unhappy with your job. **It's a matter of finding your niche.**

Have courage to fight for the job you want. A friend of mine was always nervous asking for more money or a promotion. Fortunately, she had a husband who had enough courage for the both of them, and he advised her each step of the way: from getting the money to study for her PhD to getting paid what she was worth. She was always encouraged by her husband. And she was always successful in getting what she deserved.

Be Sure Your Promotion Is Real

I started my own business after I saw I was at a dead end in the company I was working for. I had received a "shallow" promotion with a title that sounded great, but with no professional ladder to climb to make more money. Too late, I discovered it was really not a promotion because I lost my seven-person staff and the management responsibility that entailed. Thankfully, one gentleman in another department (whom I respected immensely) told me the "facts of life": I was going nowhere in the company. You need a friend like I had, or a mentor who can look out for you. In this case, I discovered I had both.

Later on, I heard from the wife of the former vice president of my former company's division. She confided that my boss and her husband had set me up, knowing I would never "make it" in this corporation—my personality would not allow me to thrive in the corporate bureaucracy. It confirmed what I had suspected was the case, after my boss' executive assistant once told me that my boss was afraid I would take his job!

Although my mother and father continued to push me, I guess my mother knew what she was saying when she said, "If only you were a boy." Yes, if only I were a boy, I could have majored in corporate finance and gone to Wall Street, and possibly made lots of money, like the other "boys" in my Wharton School class did. (If you recall, I mentioned earlier that I was *not permitted* to major in corporate finance by the department head, so I went to the marketing department chair; he agreed to take me.) Who knows? Maybe I would have hated Wall Street. But I never had the chance to find out. I took the path that was open to me, of majoring in marketing, a field that was beginning to open up to women.

In the early 1980s, on a ski trip to Jackson Hole, I met several young men who had given up Wall Street—they were burned out. Maybe I would have burned out, too. But it would have been nice to be allowed to try.

I never thought about gender issues when I began work... wow, was I naïve. It's only now that I realize I didn't "qualify" for some jobs because I was a woman. Even "tests" were stacked against me. (I stopped taking them.) If someone wanted to hire me, they would have to make the decision without the tests. This is where paying your dues and showing results for your work come in. Be sure you document your results.

Don't be naïve. Keep your eyes wide open when you job hunt. *Find the best career path you can. Then do the best job you can do to succeed.* If there is a man or woman who can mentor you, this is a connection to cultivate. Mentors are so important. Look for a man or woman who can help you in your career. Be sure you do not have any emotional involvement with this person or you will not receive objective advice. Be sure your mentor is interested only in your career. Then follow his or her advice.

Quick tip: Learn to read upside-down. One time, I had a job interview, and the interviewer had a memo on his desk specifying the salary range. I was able to read it upside-down and see the salary range. I asked for a figure in the middle of the range. Looking back, I think I should have gone for the top of the range!

CHAPTER 6

Surviving in the Corporate Environment

The corporate environment is a tough one to succeed in, especially if you are a woman. Before you decide to take a job in a large corporation, or even if you're already working in one, there are a number of questions you should ask yourself, to make sure this is the path you want to follow.

Search the Internet

The first question usually has to do with pay. What is the appropriate salary for you? The best way to find out, obviously, is to determine what others in the same company, or same industry or same job, are making. Fortunately, finding that out these days is much easier than it was when I was starting out in my career. We didn't have the internet back then. You do. Take advantage of it.

There is a great deal of information about salaries available on the web. A simple online search like "How do I know what I should be paid" will yield a plethora of advice and information that will guide you in determining what you should ask for and how to negotiate for the best result.

Once you get to the stage where you're offered the job, look at the pay you're being offered. Is the salary offered way too high, or way too low based on your research? Then be careful. Try to find out the reason for the disparity and decide whether it makes sense. Some companies want to diversify their staff and offer more money to women. Other women want to start their careers and will take less salary.

Find out everything you can about the particular company you are considering. You can choose any company you want to work for, but take a good look around to understand what you may be getting yourself into. Is there an unspoken rule that you have to work a certain number of years to earn a promotion or you will be asked to leave—the old "up or out" rule? At other companies, your ability to bring in new business is important.

As I have said elsewhere in this book, I was very naïve in choosing the companies I worked for. I was always simply looking for the company that would make me happy and pay me more money. I didn't think about much else. There was no choice. But you should understand the challenges you may face when you select a company to work for. When you're being interviewed, be ready to ask questions. *If the person you ask is offended by the question, that may be a sign you might not want to work there anyway.*

If the job you're considering would require a move across the country, or even to another city, do a thorough search on the company. What is its reputation? What is being said about it? Are there articles about discrimination at this company? Spend the time (and money, if necessary) to find out as much as you can about the company. Through the internet, search the name of the company. Arrange to visit the company for an in-person interview so you can get a better feel of the situation. Are you being taken seriously? Is this an appropriate position for you?

At the company you're considering joining, is there a career path for women? Are women promoted on merit? What are the criteria for a promotion? Is there a level playing field? Are you looking at a company with only younger women? Of course if you are looking at something like an information technology company, that is a younger person's business so you probably won't find many older women. But in other fields, you'll want to see women at various levels of the corporate hierarchy so you can tell whether this is a place where you can advance and make a career for yourself. Are there routes for a STEM (Science, Technology, Engineering, Mathematics) graduate? What are they? There should be many routes for you. If not, maybe this is the wrong company for you.

Find out what you have to do to achieve the success you want. There are still too many gender stereotypes out there, but we are seeing more and more women who are "making it." *You can make it too, if you use your head and ask the right questions.*

Why Are You Not Being Promoted?

If you're already working in a company but you're not advancing the way you think you should, try to figure out why. Is there someone standing in your way? Talk with your manager first, then if you receive an unsatisfactory response, move up the line or go the HR department. (In our time, fifty years ago, we considered the human resources department not worthy of our effort—but today, it is the court of last resort in many companies. These days, HR departments are generally much more responsive.) Finally, consider if it is time for you to look for another company where you'll have more opportunity for advancement.

If the man standing in your way is known for his inability to promote women, find a mentor who can go to the man's boss, or find a coach who can show you how to succeed. If upper management supports and promotes women, this is a good sign, but don't be impressed if too many of the women you see on the executive floor are executive assistants. There is nothing wrong with being an executive assistant—many women who started out as secretaries are promoted to these jobs because they are competent, efficient, and discrete. But what you want to see are women in executive positions, not executive assistants.

There are still some companies that are not welcoming to women. Some will find ways to say, "Women are too emotional." You always must look, act, and speak professionally. Women want to do the "right thing," but be sure you are responding to help the company. Have your reasons logically thought out.

Stop saying, "I'm sorry," when you appear emotional. Do not argue every time you don't agree. There are many articles and books written about "emotional" women. Men seem to have the advantage when they are angry. They are thought to be strong and decisive. Women do not have the same leeway, so THINK before you speak.

Responding to Demeaning Comments

What should you do if your boss makes sexist or disparaging remarks about you? My advice is NOT to let it go. You don't have to be obnoxious about it, but find a way to make your point. I once made a presentation to a group of men. When I completed my presentation, I asked the men in the room to give me a chance to work with each of them on public relations programs—I might not always have the time. I recall saying "don't push me; I will do the best I can." That's when my boss told the group of men seated around the table: "I wonder how far the old broad will go?" When we left the room, instead of yelling at him, I tried a pointed but more conciliatory approach. I told my boss that when he put me down, he put down the entire team. He never uttered a negative word again.

Don't let such incidents go; stand up for yourself. Use the assertive approach. You can say something like, "I saw what you did" or "I heard what you said"… "I assume you meant no harm or disparagement, but in the future, I would appreciate it if…" and then explain what behavior would be more appropriate. You worked hard your entire life to get to this point; do not give up on your career. But if this man continues to belittle you and will not help you, no matter what you do, should you be wasting your time at this job?

Raising Your Voice

Sometimes no matter what you do, you will have to raise your voice to make your point. You can still be feminine but don't hesitate to be strong. You don't have to be "tough" to succeed in your chosen field. Yet, as women, sometimes we feel there is not much we can do except "go along to get along." If that means you have to be someone you do not want to be, you will never be happy.

Sometimes, you do have to be tough—or at least assertive. I remember one time receiving a bonus check that was so small it was pitiful. I had worked hard in a new financial communications program; I had started a five-minute financial radio program for senior investment officers twice a day, at the opening and closing of the stock market. I had also made some major inroads for senior officers to be quoted in major national financial media. I recall going into my senior vice president's office and throwing the paltry bonus check back on his desk, saying "You obviously need this more than I do." I was so upset with the small bonus that I just did not care what happened to me. The senior vice president asked me to give him a month. He told me that he valued me and wanted to do better.

I remember vividly my response: "If that is the ball game you want to play, then I'll play by your rules." In other words, "I've made my point, let's see what you will do." Within the month, I had received a second promotion along with a much more respectable check.

OK, it worked that time; sometimes it won't. Had I overvalued myself? I did not think so then and I don't think so now. I look back and think about my mother who told me, **"If you know you are correct, say so!"** I felt I had earned my bonus and promotion, and my boss ultimately agreed. But you should not demand things you have not truly earned.

If you see or hear men berating women or hear women berating other women, then the company and the job may not be for you. Everyone is "expected" to be nice the first time you meet them. Go back for the second time and develop very good questions to find out if you will survive in this environment. If there are too many levels of hierarchy in the company, is this the place you want to be? Will you be able to reach the higher levels? If you are happy "fitting in," then you probably will be all right.

Is It Time to Move On?

What if you don't achieve the promotion you are seeking? **Do not be tempted to "sleep your way to the top."** We all have heard about the infamous Hollywood casting couch. In most places that's passé, but it still exists. Think Harvey Weinstein or Roger Ailes. So stop. You do not want to get a reputation that this is all you are good for. That would be is a huge mistake you will regret.

Look around in your company and see who has been promoted. Be generous in your evaluation to determine if the woman deserved the promotion. If you have the courage, ask the person who received the promotion what she did to earn it. Chances are, she will tell you. Assuming the woman did earn the promotion, ask yourself what you have to change to be more like this woman? What is she sacrificing, if anything? Are you willing to make that same sacrifice? Do you have talents similarly worthy of a promotion? If so, you should say something to someone who can consider your promotion.

Sometimes leaving your company is the only move you can make. I have said this before… A decade ago, moving around a lot was a sign of instability; now, everyone expects young people to move when the situation warrants, and to find her niche. So don't be timid if you find you made a mistake in selecting the company you chose. Just make sure you don't jump from the frying pan into the fire when you choose another company. Check with your friends, or whomever you know who can give you an assessment; just decide if you can trust the person or not. If you can't trust the person you ask for an assessment, find someone else to ask. In fact, ask several people. Then you can be more sure of your decision whether to stay or to leave.

Chapter 6 Summary

Surviving in the Corporate Environment—Some questions to ask yourself

- How do I know what I should be paid? Too low? Too high? Search the internet.
- How long do I have to wait to earn a promotion? Is there a promotion system I should know about?
- Are there too many levels of hierarchy? What are they? How likely is it that I will be able to reach one of the top levels?
- Is this company welcoming for women?
- Are women promoted to upper level positions?
- Is there a mentor or a coach who can assist me?
- Can I stand up for myself?
- Are women only promoted if they sleep their way to the top?
- Are men condescending toward women?
- Are women condescending toward other women?
- Do I find that I don't know myself anymore? Am I acting like someone I don't want to be?
- Should I stay or leave?

CHAPTER 7

Starting Your Own Business

Sometimes, no matter what you do, you will never be happy working for someone else or in a large company. If you're in that situation, and you are thinking seriously about starting your own business, my advice is to go for it! I did, and it was a great experience for me.

The Telltale Signs

I worked in corporations for 16 years, but at the last one, a large Fortune 100 company, I realized I was not suited for the rules, regulations, and politics of the corporate environment. I wanted to do things "my way." I always was unhappy having to bite my tongue and not say what I was really thinking. At one point, I was given a new boss but it was clear to me that he was under the influence of my former boss. After having been at the company for more than three years, all the while receiving excellent performance reviews, I suddenly received one that was terrible, essentially cutting me off from any future promotion or salary increase. It was very discouraging, since the review indicated that despite my previous success, I would now have to work harder than ever. I would have to keep my mouth shut and love my existing boss. Based on the comments he made, I decided it was time to leave.

That's when I began thinking about starting my own business. I took a long walk with my father on a Maryland beach and told him about my situation. He asked me, "What do you have to lose?" I replied, "nothing." He said he would help me, so I left the company and went into business for myself. My husband supported my decision as well.

A Partner?

At first, the plan was for a coworker and I both to leave at roughly the same time and start a business together. Both of us were discontented in the corporate environment. So, I prepared everything we would need on the expectation that we would have a partnership—logo, letterhead, business cards, agreement, and so on. Unfortunately, the partnership failed before it ever got started. My partner suddenly decided she did not want to leave and she rededicated herself to her job. I seriously wanted to get out of the corporate world and start my own business. Part of the motivation was that I wanted to have more control over my time and consider having children. (Ironically, about a year later, my once-envisioned partner did leave her job to start a family. I, on the other hand, was never able to have children, so I put all my energy into my business, working harder than I ever had in corporate life.)

The Departure

I knew I had to be careful about how I would announce my departure. I made arrangements to meet with my boss (actually, at that point, he was technically my boss's boss). I knew he loved chocolate, so I thought I would invite him to a nearby restaurant for hot chocolate. You have no idea how difficult it was to find hot chocolate 35 years ago in downtown Philadelphia! I finally found a hotel that would serve hot chocolate and I made an appointment to meet my boss's boss there.

Before I met with him, I spoke with the executive assistant to the chairman of the company, to give her a "head's up" on my plan to leave. She and my boss's boss were good friends, so I knew she would tell him. When I later met with my boss's boss, it was clear he knew what I was going to say and had thought through what he wanted to say and do. When I told him I was starting my own business, he offered to hire me as an independent contractor for a year at a decent monthly retainer. He even told me that if it turned out I didn't like being on my own, I could return to the company after the year. Of course, I never went back. In fact, my one-year retainer kept getting renewed by another department and this turned into seven years of work for my former company. I ran my firm for 35 years until I retired!

Starting Out

Once I started my own business (it was a public relations firm), my business network (about 500 people back then) really proved its worth. I developed a professionally-printed mailer on card stock, sized to fit into a standard #10 business envelope (this format is called a "slim jim" in the printing trade). The services I offered were shown on the front, underneath my nascent company's logo. My biographical sketch was printed on the back. I called a woman who had once worked as my intern and asked her if she would type addresses onto 500 envelopes. She agreed. (I don't remember what I paid her, but I'm sure it was fair at the time.) I then wrote personal notes on each of the cards, put them in the envelopes and mailed them to all my contacts. The mailing was very successful; I attracted four additional clients from that mailing.

Soon, another woman I knew called me; she was crying and said she had to quit her job because she was pregnant and couldn't keep up the job's hectic schedule. Would I take her on for a couple of days a week? I was happy to do this, and she was willing to work at a price I could afford. Another professional woman with whom I was a friend asked me if I would like a secretary who was looking for three days a week of work. I said yes to that, too. So, with two employees and myself, I started my firm.

I don't think I realized back then how much work it is to start a business. (The man who bought my business when I retired 35 years later got the benefit of all my hard work, everything I had learned and all the systems we developed over those thirty-five years.)

I decided to run the business out of my home. (Fortunately, the zoning laws in the town where we lived were not an obstacle.) I couldn't afford any "real" office space at that time, not even in suburban South Jersey, let alone downtown Philadelphia. The Delaware River is a psychological barrier to some business people in Philadelphia, so we joked to prospective clients that we could arrange for a green card for them to come across the river to New Jersey.

Fortunately, we had a four-bedroom house, so my husband and I turned our basement into an office. The staff gradually grew. So, then it became the basement and one of the bedrooms. Then the basement and two bedrooms. Then the basement, two bedrooms and the kitchen!

Once I began to find work papers left in my powder room and on my kitchen counter, I decided it was time to move out of the house and into leased office space. By that time, I knew I had enough retainers to last for six months, so I asked my husband—who had left his law firm and joined me full time by that point—to look for office space outside the home. (One of the reasons why my husband left his law practice was that his mentor worked 70 billable hours a week; he eventually left his wife and two children. Yes, he became chair of his firm and did quite well.)

Computer Equipment, an Office and My Husband, the Attorney

Starting out, we needed some office equipment. A woman who worked at my former company gave me an electric typewriter the company was getting rid of. She was tasked with donating equipment to nonprofit organizations. I certainly was not making a profit at the beginning, so she was comfortable giving me one of the typewriters.

My father loaned me some stock so I could put it up as collateral for a bank loan to buy an Apple II+ computer (the IBM PC had just been introduced and did not yet have the breadth of accessories and software that the Apple had at that point). We also got two 5¼-inch floppy drives, a "letter quality" daisy wheel printer, a word processing program, and a spreadsheet program. All told, that system (with a whopping 64 kilobytes of memory!) cost $7,600. I paid this loan off as quickly as I could, making sure I could cover my staff expenses first. I was also able to buy a second-hand copier cheaply, directly from the company that had sold the equipment originally.

The frugality I adopted paid off handsomely. I was able to hire a writer three days a week. My husband could not have been a better person to have on my side. He was practicing law during the day, then coming home to edit my work in the evening. He also bought and set up the computer system. Later, he wrote a time and billing program (imitating the one they had at his law firm) and a database program to manage our mailing lists. He kept improving those programs as our needs expanded, and we used them for over 30 years.

Work, Work, Work

Remember, you have to keep a positive outlook—failure was never an option for me. One lesson I learned is that you don't want to have your out-of-home office too close to your home (my first office was a mere one and one-half miles from our home). Otherwise, you will be there all the time—a natural tendency when you have a business is to work all the time. Once we moved our firm to a second office, farther away from my home (about nine miles), I didn't go there as often during nonbusiness hours; instead, I took work home with me (not much better but it saved on driving time). It was nothing to be on email at midnight.

When my husband and I rented a place at the Jersey shore in 1989 for half of the summer, we wouldn't get to our shore place until 2 am on Friday morning because we were working late at the office on Thursday evening. Then, we would work all weekend (we had a computer and portable fax machine at the condo), and finally, go back to the office early on Monday morning. This lasted for four summers, when we finally decided to call a halt to it because we were doing nothing but working all the time.

The Accounts

I began my business with relatively small, easy projects; as we got bigger, we began handling more complex projects. The first big account we landed was because of a friend who knew another friend who knew the chief executive officer of the organization (see, your network connections are important.). The date of our first pitch was set for when I was in Europe. I sent my first employee to Detroit. She was nervous and scared. She won that account; it was a great morale booster for her to pitch and win the account (we had that account for 27 years).

Another big account we won was when a major PR firm arrived at the pitch meeting with several people, including its chief executive officer. But that CEO left the meeting well before it was over. The client's decision maker was furious that the CEO cared so little about the account. We won that account—one that was instrumental in growing our business. Years later, a third account we won was an international organization that chose us because of the international network of firms we had joined. We already had a good track record and, with a good international network, we beat out a worldwide firm to win this client. This account is still with my former firm.

The Clients We Lost

Chemistry was great for all three accounts, but no matter how good the chemistry, we lost a few potential clients, too. *To try to find out what we could do better to win such accounts, we hired a management consultant.* He told us coming in second was just as bad as coming in ninth, so he contacted the accounts we lost and asked why. What I learned was that I had to stop making all the pitches myself; that I should not sound so dictatorial when I recommended programs; and that our firm should learn more about a prospective client before making the pitch.

Enough About Me

So what do you need to do to start a business?

The foundation is your overwhelming desire to start your own business and your strong work ethic. *Then you need an idea or a skill that sets you apart from others in your category. You also need a great network of contacts.*

You'll need office equipment, including a computer and a printer, along with a cell phone and a postage machine and scale. (Of course, these days internet access is an absolute must.) (*See* Exhibit 7.1.)

Depending upon the type of company you decide to open, you may need a good friend or spouse who can critique your sales pitch and edit anything you've written, an IT specialist to help you set up your computer system, and an inexpensive marketing or ad agency. Can you barter for any of these services?

You also should assemble a group of freelancers and consultants who are in the same business as you to help you during overload times. Don't hire freelancers who do exactly the same thing as you do, or you will risk losing your clients; you want people who offer services that complement yours. Pay your consultants fairly, in line with the level of service they are providing—maybe the same level as you are.

Exhibit 7.1 Basic things you need to start a service business

- Letterhead and envelopes—you can start with a #10 business envelope, then later purchase 6 × 9 and then 11 × 14 envelopes as needed. For the larger envelopes, you can consider return address stickers to keep the costs down.
- Business cards—make sure they are legible
- Company brochure
- Agreement letter or contract
- Computer
- Printer (preferably laser, not inkjet)
- Copier/scanner—consider an MFP (multifunction printer), which combines a printer, copier, and scanner in one unit. Again, the printer component should be laser, not inkjet.
- Postage meter
- Time and billing program—many useful time and billing programs can be found on the internet. Make sure to select one that matches the way your company will work.
- Mailing list—good but simple mailing list programs are hard to find. You may need an information technology person for this.
- Internet access
- Any other equipment you'll need to manufacture a product or provide a service.

Some Other Things You Need Before You Start Your Business
- A great idea
- A good network of contacts
- An attorney, CPA, printer, and marketing or ad agency—find the best you can afford.
- An advisory board
- A stable of good freelancers
- A banker who understands your business
- A contact at the Small Business Administration (SBA)
- A contact at your local chamber of commerce. Make an appointment to meet the CEO. (I started out on the communications committee.)

It is also an excellent idea to establish an advisory group who can counsel you or give you advice on business strategy and problem-solving.

Continue learning as much as you can. I took one of the first classes in crisis communications. I became an expert. I also joined another organization where I met an environmental engineer. As I mentioned before, I teamed up with his engineering firm and, before I realized it, I had combined my crisis communications expertise with environmental communications. I read a lot and went to lectures given by a guru in the environmental communications arena. From there, I learned community relations, since we had to tell the community what they needed to know about a crisis or an environmental situation. One thing led to another; as my business grew from crisis response to crisis preparedness, the community relations part grew bigger as did spokesperson training. My advice is to keep learning from every situation where you find yourself challenged.

The bottom line is that you should not feel you are "stuck" in a corporate environment, if you dislike it. Go ahead, start your own business. But **remember, you will not be a great success overnight.** As a business owner, you may not be one of the first people to arrive in the morning, but you will definitely be the last one to leave at night (my husband and I used to joke that the definition of "owner" was the person who turned off the lights and locked the doors at night). You'll water the plants and keep the office looking neat. You'll do the entertaining, and make plans to take clients out to dinner. You'll work with a management consultant on how to grow your business and manage your staff. And you'll make the lists of birthday and holiday cards to send. You will also be responsible for your company's newsletter.

You Don't Have to Do It Alone

Slowly you will grow your business and find that **you will not have to do it all alone**; at some point, you *won't be able* to do it all alone. If they have any interest, consider asking a spouse/partner or a friend to join you.

But be careful not to grow too fast by taking on customers or clients that don't fit your business model. And don't invest in a "rich-looking" office, displaying all sorts of technology. Keep the technology out of sight. *With a showy office, your clients or prospects may think you are already doing so well that you don't need their business.*

Grow your company big enough so you don't have to take on all the responsibility yourself (My husband joined me to help run our business by handling the accounting and the technology). Growing a business is not easy, especially when you encounter a recession. I started my business in a recession (I didn't even realize it at the time), so it was a challenge. We also faced the tech bubble of the late '90s, followed by 9/11/2001. And then the banking crisis of 2008–2009. There were several recessions in between, so it wasn't easy. But looking back, we think it was worth it. Keep going, recession or boom. You will have to work harder during a recession but the principles are the same.

Retirement

When you are ready to retire, try to sell your business during a boom time when your sales are higher. **Think hard about whether you will retire as soon as you sell your business, or whether you are prepared to stay on with the company under the new owner.** If you have a service firm built on your reputation, do your best to groom a successor and build a transition to the new leadership. Put yourself in the background and put your successor out front.

Ask questions of colleagues before you are ready to sell; get a lot of advice. My husband's legal background, plus information we received from our colleagues at similar companies, helped us to develop a strategy to sell the firm to our senior employee gradually over a period of years. Every two years, we worked one day less each week, but we set our salaries to stay the same over the transition period. Our salaries were based on the sale price, not on our work schedule. That strategy may not work for everyone, but it certainly did for us.

I started a business that lasted 35 years until I retired. Since retirement, my husband and I travel as much as we can. I am the "social" person in our small family, so I have made many friends over the years. Most of them don't live anywhere near us, but that will just give us an excuse to travel when we want to go see them!

Afterword

It's great to see and reflect upon how far women have come; but we understand the challenges women still continue to face. From her years of experience as the founder of Diversified Search, and as the founder of the Forum of Executive Women in Philadelphia, Judith von Seldeneck, offered these comments in my book "*On the Cusp*":

> Women in business have come a long way since the sixties, but obviously not as far as we would like. Some of the old traditional obstacles remain, but they are dwindling with passage of time. There has never been a better time for women who truly want to excel in their careers to do so. But they have to be willing to make their careers their top priority, and commit the time and energy and go toe to toe with the best and the brightest!
>
> There are no free rides; there never have been. But the highways are newly paved and the vehicles equipped to excel at a record pace. Women now need to step up and get behind the controls.[1]

Women should not give up. There are many decisions to make along the way. I hope this book helps women make those decisions about their careers, their lives and their futures.

—Anne S. Klein

---

[1] Klein, A.S. 2018. *On The Cusp: The Women of Penn '64*, 181. Pine Road Press.

References Online for Women Seeking Careers

Times have changed only a little bit for working women over the past 50 years. But it's still tough in the business world, even though the 1993 Family and Medical Leave Act made life a little easier, allowing for women (or for their husbands/partners) to take off up to 12 weeks to care for a new child (natural-born or adopted), care for a seriously ill family member, or recover from a serious illness.

Still among the most common women's careers are nursing, teaching and secretarial. But those aren't the only choices, by far. "In 2017, women accounted for 52 percent of all workers employed in management, professional, and related occupations, somewhat more than their share of total employment (47 percent). The share of women in specific occupations within this large category varied. For example, 19 percent of software developers, 28 percent of chief executives, and 40 percent of physicians and surgeons were women, whereas 90 percent of registered nurses, 79 percent of elementary and middle school teachers, and 60 percent of accountants and auditors were women."[1]

If you're searching for a career, you will find online any number of articles that have been written for women on a variety of subjects, many of which are included in this book. For example, *Forbes, Harvard Business Review, the New York Times, CNBC,* Vault.com and AOL.com, among others, have many articles on women and careers. There also are articles listed in 2020 Daily Muse, the Pew Research Center, and the US Department of Labor. You also can find women's jobs and issues faced in *USAToday.com*, researchgate.net, thebalancecareers.com, mscareergirl.com, fairygodboss.com, Monster.com and The Voice of Job Seekers (podcasts).

---

[1] BLS Reports: Women in the labor force: a databook (December 2018). https://bls.gov/opub/reports/womens-databook/2018/home.htm

The easiest way to find such articles is by simply using your favorite internet search engine (e.g. Google, Bing, Yahoo, Baidu, Yandex, DuckDuckGo and numerous others). Search for topics like Women and Business Careers, Women and Careers, Women's Careers, Nontraditional Careers for Women, Women and Work, Women in the Workplace, and Businesswomen in the Workplace. Customize your search for your own particular career interests. Online research is also very helpful for women who want to work part-time once they have a family.

There are many full books on these subjects, but many of them illustrate how difficult life can be when you are a woman pursuing a career. You should have a lot of courage and confidence, and the right partner or spouse who will support your career efforts. Books you might want to read include *Dare to Dream* by Whitney Johnson, *Girl Boss* by Sophia Amoruso, *Leave Your Mark* by Aliza Licht, *Lean In* by Sheryl Sandburg and *Lean Out* by Marissa Orr. Businessinsider.com lists the best career books for women. There are too many books to list here, but if you look, you are sure to find a book on any subject that appeals to you.

One particular author I found to be a great resource is Stephen Covey, author of *The 7 Habits of Highly Effective People, First Things First, Principle Centered Leadership, Living the Seven Habits, Seven Habits for Managers*, and many more. There are older books like *Games Mother Never Taught You* by Betty Lehan Harragan and *Men and Women of the Corporation* by Rosabeth Moss Kanter. The last two books were of my generation, but still have good lessons in them for today.

Many colleges and universities have Women's Programs and Women's Studies. If you are a student at the college, you should ask for assistance at the career center or, if you're a graduate, talk with your alumni office.

Considering that references change all the time (and can quickly become out of date), we can't give you an exhaustive list, but we think the aforementioned suggestions will get you started in the right direction.

Addendum

The NEW Normal

I wrote this book in four months, while I was at home during the 2020 Covid-19 "stay-at-home" timeframe. Some things have changed, and we have no idea when we will return to the "normal" as we knew it. As of this writing, life is starting to return to "normal," but it does not feel the same.

Many of us were able to work remotely, using our laptop computers and our phones. But for those women who were seeking to get started in their careers or move on in their careers, job hunting has changed.

Job hunting became a challenge, unless you had a job or an internship you loved and your employer loved you. You might have been offered a position last year or over the winter. Take it to get started with your career. If you were thinking about moving on in your career, this may not be the time to begin looking. If you are looking for an advancement or a new career, read on.

Word-of-mouth marketing is increasing in its value. There is a Word-of-Mouth Professional Marketing Association (WOMMA) that began several years ago. In a Zoom video conversation recently, a group of career women I know wondered if networking ever will return to normal. The way to network now is to join webinars where you will meet others on Zoom or Skype calls. You'll meet new people that way. In fact, the smaller the group, the more chance you will have to meet new people. I met a new woman recently in a Zoom conference call. She worked with a friend of mine, so we had a "connection." Even if you don't have a connection, at the end of the call, ask a "new" friend if you could call her or email her. Chances are, you can start a "new" connection.

Email or call everyone you know when you have to job hunt. Accept new people who want to "connect" or "friend" you on LinkedIn or Facebook. Connect with anyone who wants to connect with you on Instagram, Twitter or Parler. You can't afford to ignore anyone (unless you have no interest whatsoever, or the person wants to "friend" you because you are "pretty") because you don't know who they know.

Your skill in looking sharp or sounding intelligent on a phone call or a video interview will be invaluable. Hone your skills practicing a conversation with a parent, sibling, spouse, or partner. Once you are hired, even if it's remotely, show your value. Resist the urge to surf the internet or send an e-mail to a friend; it's so easy to do so when you are at home.

If you have to hire a recruiter, hire one. You can be sure the recruiter has a broader network than you have.

This is the time to be sure you have excelled in your studies. Unless you have the right "connection" or have been introduced by a friend, the hiring manager will have no choice but to determine your contribution to the company based on your grades.

It's a whole new world; everything has changed. As a Chinese fortune cookie reminded me: "Anything you do, do it well. The last thing you want is to be sorry for what you didn't do."

About the Author

Anne Sceia Klein, APR, Fellow PRSA

Anne S. Klein is the founder of Anne Klein Communications Group, LLC (AKCG), a firm she headed for 35 years. Anne played a leading role in the public relations arena, both in the Philadelphia region and nationally, for more than five decades. She spent 16 years in the corporate world (including the banking and oil industries) before founding her public relations firm in 1982. A counselor to top management, she has been recognized as an expert in strategic planning, crisis and issues communications, and community outreach.

Anne has been recognized with numerous awards for her outstanding achievements and contributions to her profession and to business. In 2004, Anne was inducted into the Philadelphia Public Relations Association's Hall of Fame, and in 2006, she was inducted to Rowan University's Public Relations Hall of Fame. In 2017, Anne was honored with a Lifetime Achievement Award from the Philadelphia Chapter of the Public Relations Society of America.

Under Anne's leadership, AKCG won dozens of awards for excellence in public relations. She is the author of chapters in several books and countless articles on public relations. She coauthored *On the Cusp: The Women of Penn '64* with Vilma Barr.

A graduate of The Wharton School of the University of Pennsylvania with a bachelor's degree in economics, Anne received her master's degree in communications from Penn's Annenberg School. She is an Accredited Member (APR) and a Fellow of the Public Relations Society of America.

Anne lives with her husband and former business partner, Jerry, in Medford, New Jersey. She is a past chair of the Central and Southern New Jersey region of the American Heart Association. She is also a past president of her shore condominium association and a member of the Union League of Philadelphia.

Index

www.ingramcontent.com/pod-product-compliance
Lightning Source LLC
Chambersburg PA
CBHW061838220326
41599CB00027B/5322